A True History Of Adam and Eve

The Genetic Basis for the Historicity of Adam and Eve

A True History
Of
Adam and Eve

The Genetic Basis for the Historicity of Adam and Eve

Joseph Baker

Acknowledgments

Heart Felt Gratitude is directed to King James who made possible the King James Version (KJV) translation of the Bible for the common man and woman.

Introduction

Combining the plain reading of the Book of Genesis and the latest findings, from genetic research into the human genome, the author makes a compelling case for the consistency and coherence of the Bible beginning at the very beginning of Genesis as being a true historical account of the six days of creation and the reality of the existence of Adam and Eve, being the most ancient ancestors of all of humankind that begins with the supernatural creation of Adam and Eve by God, as beings especially endowed with the unique Spirit of God (in His image).

Additionally, an account of the current state of humankind and our environment is presented by combining the implications of our current understanding of genetics and relevant Scriptural references.

Contents

Chapter 1 The First Couple

According to Genesis Adam and Eve were created directly by God, giving rise to the human race. This was a supernatural event and cannot be explained by application of the scientific method. However, the latest research into Genetics supports the unique nature of humanity and the timeline as presented in the Genesis account.

While many, in this time of scientific domination by secular interests, may find it difficult to accept Genesis as plainly read, this book will reveal that, in a substantial way, the science behind Genetics has caught up with the Biblical account found in Genesis.

This is indeed good news as Genesis provides the historical foundation for the rest of the Bible.

And Adam called his wife's name Eve; because she was the mother of all living. Genesis 3:20 (KJV)

And hath of one blood all nations of men for to dwell on all the face of the earth, and hath determined the times before appointed, and the bounds of their habitation;

For in Him we live, and move, and have our being; as certain also of your own poets have said, For we are also His offspring. Acts 17:26,28 (KJV)

Eve is the biological mother of all of humanity. Adam's legacy is similar, with one exception. Adam is the biological father of all of humanity with the exception of Jesus of Nazareth. Jesus was fathered by the Holy Spirit. We acknowledge that Adam and Eve were created by God at the end of the of the supernatural creation period on the sixth day of creation.

Everyone can trace their family tree starting from Adam and Eve or God if you like, and we all share in a common paternity up through Noah of ten generations. All nations of men are of one blood, one race: the human race. There are no apes in our family tree.

The story of Adam and Eve (and their children) herein portrayed is the true story and historical account by the plain reading of the Biblical text.

And is correlated with the latest genetic research along with other external evidences for the literal truth of the historical narrative and supreme authority of the Bible; the aim of which is to restore, establish, strengthen or confirm the Biblical World View in the heart and mind of the reader.

Chapter 2 Biblical World View

A Biblical/Christian World View is one that takes the Bible literally or naturally in the appropriate context and applies it in all aspects of daily life.

The Bible stands alone: inerrant, inspired, unchanging and God breathed. Inerrancy demonstrated by fulfilled prophecy. Inspiration solves coordinating 40 some authors of diverse social standing over centuries of time through diverse traditions and cultures; unchanging because of an infinite transcendent agency, knower of the end before the beginning. God breathed identifies the ultimate author, the perfect eternal living Godhead.

The Bible is internally consistent and declares itself to be the word of God. There are also external evidences of the truth of the Bible: personal experience such as the born again experience (spiritual birth).

Archeology and science affirm the Bible. So do eye witnesses to miracles and most of all: fulfilled prophecy, the most astounding might be Isaiah 53, seven hundred years before the crucifixion:

But He was wounded for our transgressions, He was bruised for our iniquities: the chastisement of our peace was upon Him; and with His stripes we are healed. Isaiah 53:5 (KJV)

My God, My God, why hast Thou forsaken Me?

All that see Me laugh Me to scorn: they shoot out the lip, they shake the head saying,

He trusted on the LORD that He would deliver Him: let Him deliver Him seeing He delighted in Him. Psalm 22:1a,7-8 (KJV)

The old testament predicts, with stunning accuracy, what has taken place in the new testament.

The purpose of the Bible is to lead sinners to salvation, confirmed by the bodily Resurrection of Jesus Christ, the single most important event in human history.

In order to properly understand the historicity and context of Adam and Eve it is necessary to start at the beginning of the creation account in Genesis 1 to establish the foundation of the Biblical account upon which the entire Bible depends.

Ultimately, faith in the Bible is trust in the trustworthiness of God. This faith stands alone and exceeds human expressions and opinions; and deservedly so for trusting God comes with knowing God personally, the necessary goal of all Christians. See Matthew 25:12.

Faith in the Bible is not blind. This faith is based on knowledge. The more knowledge in this regard, greater is the potential faith. Evidence based on honest truths must accumulate to reasonably support the faith in question otherwise the faith we purport might just be an irrational leap into an abyss of dark untruths, like faith in evolution, the big bang, or scientism in general.

Furthermore, to benefit beyond the intellectual knowledge of the truth of our faith there must be trust and affection for the truths the faith encapsulates for as much as God is truth God is love and our ability to have heart felt affection for God shows liking in addition to loving and is personal.

While faith comes by hearing and hearing by the word of God. If in hearing the word of God we don't accept or recognize the authority of the word of God the word will be discarded in favor of what we do accept as authoritative.

This is why skeptics argue the evidence, often distorting facts in order to confuse. Guard your heart. Listening to them is like voting for their opinion. These votes accumulate resulting in a degree of unbelief. When we are weak one vote may be enough. Guard your heart. Don't argue with fools.

Be not deceived: evil communications corrupt good manners. 1 Corinthians 15:33 (KJV)

True faith affects our behavior. It is not just an internal phenomena. We act on our true beliefs, not necessarily something we have in our mind, but in our heart.

Supernatural faith is a gift given at salvation. It is the faith of Jesus, not the faith in Jesus. This faith is accessed by belief in this faith and is the enormous faith of Jesus!

I completely, whole heartedly and enthusiastically accept the accounts of creation in Genesis, Adam and Eve and the crucifixion and bodily Resurrection of Jesus Christ. They are true, historical and factual accounts of events given for our edification.

I believe in the six literal days of creation. This comes from understanding that creation has to be a supernatural event and that the creator is a supernatural transcendent being possessing unimaginable power. The Bible clarifies this in Exodus 20:11. The context of this verse directly ties the six days of creation with the six day work week.

This text is part of the ten commandments given in Exodus 20:2-17. This is the only portion of the entire Bible written directly by the finger of God (upon two stone tablets), giving it unique significance over all and should be a warning to anyone wanting to mess with the meaning therein.

This should put a nail in the coffin of those who want to propose strange interpretations to compromise with and please the ungodly, this also questions the diligence of those who deny they can understand what God meant in Genesis 1-11.

Remember the sabbath day, to keep it holy.
Six days shalt thou labor, and do all thy work:
But the seventh day is the sabbath of the LORD thy God: in it thou shalt not do any work, thou, nor thy son, or thy daughter, thy manservant, not thy maidservant, nor thy cattle, nor thy stranger that is within thy gates:
<u>For in six days</u> the Lord made heaven and earth, the sea, and all that in them is, and rested the seventh day: wherefore the LORD blessed the sabbath, and hallowed it. Exodus 20:8-11 (KJV, emphasis mine)

Don't you think God would have known of our controversies involved in the supernatural creation of all that exists?

The creation account is a historical narrative, not a scientific account and since creation is a supernatural event it is beyond what science can explain. Trying to use science to explain creation is folly. Science is bound by the natural order, the physical laws, especially by the laws of thermodynamics; though it seems this is ignored by most astrophysicists and cosmologists in their theories.

God is transcendent of the natural order and indeed is the uncaused cause of the natural order.

How can it be any other way?

The creation account give us boundaries and chronology of God's supernatural creation, neatly confounding attempts to reinterpret by virtue of its plain reading.

There are popular authors and popular 'scientists', who with their wit and charisma promote evolution, big bangs, gaps, day age and other theories and have quite a following and best sellers but are not promoting Jesus (or the God of the Bible, Father, Son and Holy Spirit), but some other god. While they may disrepute atheism they trample all over holy scripture, succumbing to a Genesis 3 attack.

They operate under a mistaken belief that they are refuting atheists. Instead they are being fooled by Satan who is using the time tested Genesis 3 attack (see Chapter 6). One does not have to understand everything in the Bible in order to believe it. Those who think they are wise and can explain everything on their own are fools before God. Repent. I have!

Professing themselves to be wise, they became fools. Romans 1:22 (KJV)

Where is the wise? where is the scribe? where is the disputer of this world? hath not God made foolish the wisdom of this world? 1 Corinthians 1:20 (KJV)

But God hath chosen the foolish things of the world to confound the wise; 1 Corinthians 1:27a (KJV)

I believe in the historical Adam and Eve, just as the Bible reveals. There is overwhelming genetic evidence being uncovered in this regard. The Biblical account of Adam and Eve straddles the supernatural and the natural phase of the beginning of all things. The setup disclosed in the creation account is masterfully engineered with the focus being on the earthly element of the home for humanity.

I believe in the actual, bodily Resurrection of Jesus Christ. This is the final act in the resolution for the sin of Adam and Eve and the legal seizure of the earthly empire by the satan under the authority given by the treachery of Adam and Eve. This completes the manifestation of the new covenant of salvation by grace through faith doctrine, Pentecost not withstanding.

Regarding the Resurrection: There are testimonies accepted by Biblical Scholars even among unbelievers. Some may not believe in the resurrection but they do acknowledge that the witnesses believed they had encountered the Resurrected Jesus following the crucifixion. These testimonies are considered to be early and unimpeachable by many scholars for various reasons. There is astonishing physical evidence in the Shroud of Turin and substantial circumstantial evidence.

There are many recent archeological finds that suggest or confirm events described in the Bible are true, literal and happened when and how they are described. Scientific archeology has only been around for a couple of centuries and the fruits of that labor are starting to manifest, though not commonly reported to the lay person.

(1)Young earth creation geologists are making an effective effort to refute non-scientific geological assertions and give new light to allow a proper analysis of major geological evidence and events leading to conclusions that completely support those events as described in the Bible, especially the Genesis flood being a global flood of unimaginable devastation. Traces of earthquakes reported in the Bible have been found in dead sea sediments. These traces are very precise in documenting specific earthquakes which corresponds to the Biblical accounts of those events.

A plethora of science 'facts' misinterpreted or outright ignored in order to support a secular world view can be interpreted in a Biblical world view which supports a young earth creation and in some cases gives strong evidence disputing secular interpretations as highly unlikely.

In all, the Bible is found to be completely trust worthy.

I believe it is important to survey, enumerate and validate external evidences for the historicity of the Bible and to survey the internal validation of the Bible for our individual benefit and importantly to educate the next generation of believers especially given the assault from many corners of our society to destroy our Christian civilization, including from within.

Compromising with these forces in our society leads to no good end and is a faith destroyer. For our own good we need   believers to really believe beyond the point of salvation and to integrate knowledge of the truth that they may impart, through discipleship and maturation, a continual and generational tradition until Christ returns.

May God Bless our children.

Chapter 3 Before the Beginning

For God so loved the world, that He gave His only begotten Son, that whosoever believeth in Him shall not perish, but have everlasting life. John 3:16 (KJV)

Why does anything exist in the first place? How can anything exist? Without a priori motive can anything reasonably exist? In other words there has to exist outside of natural existence a transcendent motivator and a motive that would bring the natural into existence since the natural world cannot create itself and nothing can create nothing and cannot have existed forever (without everything having run down in the eternal past).

Imbedded in the manifestation there would have to be purpose to the unfolding and order of the things we observe with our five senses. This implies that the 'natural' is an emanation of the 'supernatural' under the control of a transcendent intelligent agent, this kind of agent is necessary because a priori motive and purpose can only come from such.

Nothing cannot produce anything but nothing. The natural realm could not arise accidentally of its own accord for it did not exist in the first place. Such is nonsense in the most literal form and in my way of thinking is only proposed by those who are trying to avoid God so that they can determine right from wrong by their own predilection which goes right back to the mistake made by Adam and Eve.

Imagine that.

The physical universal cannot be infinite in time past and must have had a creator; otherwise, in the infinite past every warm thing including the sun would have cooled down to the temperature of day old coffee. This is the second law of thermodynamics, aka heat death.

The riddle of existence can only be answered by motive and purpose, otherwise the cosmos would be just a jumble of random, untraceable manifestations of aimless purposelessness. In such a universe, chaos would be seen as order, indeed and not just in the minds of the insane.

Yet, we find ourselves in an ordered universe, pregnant with hidden purpose contained in the smallest living cell, being more complex than our largest factories, a microscopic entity we cannot begin to duplicate with all the resources and technology at our disposal. Though we may try we cannot even fathom how they came into being.

Thus builds the case for a supernatural God, who is responsible for everything including the very laws of nature, space, time, matter and energy, to say nothing of love, understanding, wisdom, virtue, awareness and existence.

So why did God create? What was His motive? Such a powerful being could create more than we could ever imagine. So why did He give us existence, the world and the Bible? Because He is love and we are His targets. And given the way this love is He wants us to love Him back freely, to like Him, voluntarily and in fact, He also wants us to respect HIm. We cannot do that if we don't exist. If we don't know Him we can't know His love and we can't choose, by virtue of freewill, to respond in kind! God wants us to know Him and He is a good God, faithful, holy, merciful and just.

So how did He do it? By His powerful word and will. He is all powerful and very very wise. I believe He created the foundation of the world and the whole cosmos in six literal earth days, just as He tells us in Genesis.

Why would we try to interpret it any other way? God knows more than we do, and even then about now. Only if we don't believe what He says would we seek another way.

The opinions of others can influence us. There may be legal opinions, medical opinions and so on, even scientific theories are nothing more than opinions, whereas the Holy Spirit deals in truth. Rather than reinterpretation we should ask why He did it the way He did.

Unbelief is the oldest trick in the book and the satan used it on Eve some six thousand years ago, (and continues to use it to this day). Their exchange was brief and all it took was for the satan to lie and express unbelief. Thus, by trusting the opinion of the satan (a deliberate lie, surely a warning to our own gullibility), Eve doubted God's goodness and His word and the rest is history.

Why was Eve so easily deceived?

My people are destroyed for ignorance; Hosea 4:6 (mine).

We can only avoid (this kind of) ignorance by the word of God as this was spiritual ignorance.

Do not be deceived. It should be obvious by now, but we are not near as smart as we think we are, especially those most intelligent! It seems the more intelligent we are in the flesh the more enamored we are about making up our own stories or listening to idle speculations. Especially when we want to believe a lie, for whatever reason.

Fortunate for us there is an antidote for our weaknesses and vulnerabilities. The word of God, encapsulated in the Bible, is a gift from Jesus. It is to our spirit and soul what food is to our body. We need to partake on a daily basis and guard our heart! Avoid fasting from the word.

Oh that my words were now written! oh that they were printed in a book!
That they were graven with an iron pen and lead in the rock for ever!
For I know that my redeemer liveth, and that He shall stand at the latter day upon the earth: Job 19:23-25.

Wow! looks like Job got his wish and he knew his redeemer, Jesus was already alive and would return in the latter day.

Note: a recent archeological discovery at Joshua's stone altar on Mt. Ebal: a curse on a small lead tablet, written with a stylus. This is the oldest known artifact with the names of God inscribed upon (YWH and El) and is written in proto-alphabetic Hebrew, the oldest form of Hebrew, an offshoot of ancient Egyptian hieroglyphics dating to 1400-1300BC.

This shows that there was a written language at the time of Moses, supporting the claim that Moses wrote the first five books of the old testament. He had 40 years to do it, so what's the big deal?

Chapter 4 The Foundation of the World

In the beginning God created the heavens and the earth. Genesis 1:1 (KJV)

Being clear headed how could we but accept that God is all powerful, ever present and all knowing? He exists outside of the natural realm and has complete control over it. If you believe this you should have no issue in accepting the story of creation in Genesis 1 without modification and plainly read. You would understand it much as a child would understand it, without complication.

Furthermore, once mature, you would readily discard any suggested conflicting ideas pertaining to any unproven scientific theories, contradictory philosophical world views and idle speculations.

This first Bible verse, when studied in the original Hebrew is pregnant with subtlety and such detail that a whole book could be written discussing this one verse in the context of the whole Bible. Bible study can and should be a life long pursuit for all Christians and can benefit unbelievers also as it can lead to salvation, the ultimate goal of the Bible.

The Bible came first and is unchanging; it takes precedent over the ideas of man, ideas that are speculative, constantly changing and being tweaked to conform to fit data that is often presented in biased ways that bring into question the motive of the proponents. (That some scientists can be less than honest was demonstrated by the recent pandemic. And recently it has been revealed that some Noble Laureates faked their data in papers that were subsequently peer reviewed and published, in so-called authoritative publications, thereby creating fictional shoulders for future generations to stand upon. So much for shoulders of giants. It is believed that fake scientific papers are rather common. God help us!)

What many don't know is that originally, the scientific method was an outgrowth of the belief of Biblical truth of the orderliness and precision of God's creation such that the natural world we inhabit and how it works is knowable to us. (I'm sure the earliest scientists would have found the current state of affairs intolerable. It seems that many tolerate the current state of affairs for the sake of their careers.)

There is no real conflict between a Biblical World View and honest science; indeed the scientific method found its genesis in the Biblical World View. This is historical fact.

Shockingly, secular academia has discarded the scientific method in large part in favor of a 'best in the field theory' approach. This approach purposely ignores data and findings that contradict the 'best' establishment theory unless there is a better (secular) theory to replace it. This is true even if the 'best' one is proven to be absolutely wrong!

One of the best examples of this is macro evolution of living creatures and is touted far and wide as gilded truth, but is so full of holes that it is an embarrassment. Scientists who point this out often loose their research grants and more.

Living creation was sophisticated, diverse and complete from the get go. There was no need for, nor any mention of macro evolution, millions or billions of years of earth time.

Recent genetic research supports my belief that when God created the first couple He also created the rest of humanity, stored in the vastly sophisticated DNA code of the human genome along with the support mechanisms of procreation in the germ cells of Adam and Eve giving all of the diversity we see in humanity this very day.

A supernatural kickstart by the spoken word of God is plainly revealed in the text and is the fundamental premise for a Biblical World View and the Christian faith in general.

Through faith we understand that the worlds were framed by the word of God, so that things which are seen were not made of things which do appear. Hebrews 11:3 (KJV)

The (true) story of Adam and Eve is knowable in context of a Biblical World View, without which it makes no sense, and indeed the entire Bible depends on the first three or eleven chapters of Genesis. The very foundation of human existence, morality and the meaning of life depends on a Biblical World View and an understanding of the history revealed in the Bible.

The first verse of Genesis introduces the creation of the foundation in the first act of creation of this physical universe and is the beginning of a tightly knit narrative of the six days of creation.

God created light on the first day of creation, thus illuminating the whole process of divine creation.

For the invisible things of Him from the creation of the world are clearly seen, being understood by the things that are made, Romans 1:20a-b (KJV)

Furthermore, this sequence invalidates the so called gap theory - there would have had to been light during that period which supposedly occurred before Genesis 1:2 and Genesis 1:3, when light was created.

And God said, let there be light: and there was light. Genesis 1:3 (KJV).

Notice that light was created before the sun. What creation narrative would have it in this order? Only God's narrative because that is how He did it, and He wanted us to know.

There are dozens of time bound physical phenomena that imply a young earth - on the order of 6,000 years.

No body knows (except the creator) how the moon came to be but one thing is clear: the moon is required for life to exist on earth. It can be thought of as part of the respiration, circulation, stabilization and cleansing mechanism of the earth.

The maximum age of the earth and the solar system is constrained when one considers the rate of the weakening magnetic fields of earth and other planets, rate of cooling of core temperatures of planets and moons, decay of Saturn's rings, salt and sediment content of the oceans, decay of comets, possibly the rotation of spiral galaxies, youthful appearance of the most distant galaxies, the lack of **observed** star creation (the impossibility of gravitational collapse of gaseous clouds by the laws of thermodynamics because heat generated by collapse greatly exceeds the feeble force of gravity, causing expansion to occur no matter how large is the cloud).

In spite of early successes, currently, secular cosmology and related disciplines have been relegated to fantastic models designed to keep God and the Bible out with unprovable abstract mathematics and hidden universes that can never be observed. This requires more faith than is required for a supernatural God at the helm.

All is not lost, however, as 'creation scientists' forge ahead, taking data and seeing promising results by applying a Biblical World View. One very intriguing situation is that various measurements and experiments suggest the we are at or near the center of the universe.

It's fun to watch secularists scramble to find a reinterpretation more to their liking, like the universe expanding like a balloon where there is no center on the surface. However, we can be sure the earth was the center of God's focus.

A favored tactic is to invoke a 'cosmological principle' (not even a theory, mind you) that states that there are no special places in the universe including a center; in an attempt to attribute everything to a cosmic accident of quantum fluctuations and strange geometries.

This attitude is completely counter to the Biblical world view that led to the scientific method and an unprecedented increase in scientific knowledge and the explosion of technology never before seen in the history of the world.

These facts remain: The Bible is the most accurate historical account ever penned. The Bible never gets a medical fact wrong, thousands years ahead of confirmation…

It is the glory of God to conceal a thing: but the honor of kings to search out a matter. Prov. 25:2 (KJV)

Chapter 5 The Human Family

And God said, Let us make man in our image, after our likeness; Genesis 1:26a (KJV)

Here, the special creation of humanity, from the rest of creation, is clearly stated.

Male and female create He them; Genesis 1:27c (KJV)

But from the beginning of the creation God made them male and female. Mark 10:6 (KJV)

Thus, was the foundation of the family divinely created in the very beginning. Jesus affirms this literal truth in Mark 10:6.

Current research into genetics and DNA reveal that, because of the sophisticated design of the human genome,

Adam and Eve contained in their germ cells the DNA of ALL humans, past, present and future. (Some gene sequences not present were derived from already existing genetic information found in the human genome.)

Hidden within their genetic code is the diversity of their children that we see in the world today. This diversity is not the result of mutations or evolution, but the genius behind God's design. Interactions during germ cell creation within the mother and father give rise to most variations we see today in humans (and it seems in all living creatures, within their kind).

Other factors arise within the development of offspring include environmental influences on gene expression contributing to natural selection within a given kind (of creature).

To be sure there are mutations present because this is a fallen world, and most mutations are not beneficial; this is not evolution but rather devolution. An accumulation of mutations can result in a fatal genetic combination which can occur in subsequent generations as mutations in the germ line are passed from generation to generation leading ultimately to extinction, it would seem, due to the accumulated burden of deleterious changes to the genetic code over time. The more time the worse it gets!

(6)Sometimes it takes only one mutation to cause a serious disease.

The genetic code is found in DNA and is in the form of a genetic alphabet of chemical letters, where organisms are specified in a series of words such that mutations result in random misspellings in the specification and can be corruptive and rarely if ever of benefit, can affect development, cause disease and be fatal to the organism.

These mutations are quantitatively predictable, in other words the average number of new mutations per generation is predictable at least in mtDNA and the Y chromosome, subjects of new intensive research. This predictability allows scientists to use the number of mutations as a genetic clock. This is a wonderful finding for 'creation' science and death to evolutionary biology.

As these mutations accumulate from generation to generation resulting in a degradation over time of descendants; a kind of devolution results from the disabling of genetic functions; rather than an evolution to more complex organisms or new genetic functions.

For evolution to work (since it is a random unintelligent process) much time is need to accumulate the millions of mutations for new kinds of creatures (i.e. dinosaurs changing into birds or fish changing to cats), but before millions of mutations could accumulate for this to happen, fatal mutations would occur killing off the genetic line.

Indeed, deleterious mutations are far more common than beneficial mutations. This was proven by early experiments using radiation to speed up the 'evolutionary clock'.(2) Coincidentally, many suffered from radiation poisoning before we learned to not put radium on watch hands. Note: normally, mutations are caused by copying errors during cell division and not radiation, but the genetic implications are similar and they are commonly 'single letter' mutations or point mutations.

The main difference is that mutations caused by copying errors are somewhat less destructive because of the design of the translation from DNA code to amino acid takes into account the most likely mutations such that the 'spelling error' that occurs results in a synonym that code for the same or structurally similar amino acid.

Statistics predict copying errors are most likely between DNA codes that have most similar molecular bonding energies. Understanding of this statistical fact is reflected in the design of the DNA copying process that occurs during cell duplication and show the inherent wisdom in God's design.

Given enough time all organisms are likely to go extinct because of accumulated mutations in the germ cell line!

The reason evolution was promoted in the first place was to disprove the Genesis account of creation but science has moved on and made such proposals completely false.

This includes theistic evolution. At one time I entertained this idea, but have since repented. Theistic Evolution is a modern form of syncretism. This is not science. This is atheism wrapped up in compromise.

O Timothy, keep that which is committed to thy trust, avoiding profane and vain babblings, and oppositions of science falsely so called. 1 Timothy 6:17 (KJV).

These kinds of shenanigans have been with us from the beginning as referenced in 1 Timothy 6:17.

The Genesis account gives genealogies with enough information to determine the passage of time. This calculation, from Adam and Eve until the present, gives approximately 6,000 years for mtDNA and 4500 years for the Y chromosome (4500 years to Noah for the paternal line as the Genesis flood reduced the paternal line to one individual). This also agrees with the latest DNA research done by Dr. Nathaniel T. Jeanson and others. Look him up, read his books "Replacing Darwin" and especially "Replacing Darwin Simplified" and (5)"Traced", educate your children and grand children.

There are generally two lines of research at present. One uses the maternal line of descent represented by mtDNA (mitochondrial DNA) passed from generation to generation from the mother. This DNA resides outside of the cell nucleus and is not carried by sperm cells. This DNA is involved in cellular energy production.

The second line of research uses the Y chromosome which is passed by fathers to sons only. Both of these research subjects are not subject to the mixing of maternal and paternal genes that occurs with the rest of the genome, greatly simplifying analysis.

This DNA research was possible because mutations are passed from generation to generation accumulating ancestral mutations along the way. The number of mutations is many orders of magnitude fewer than the number of DNA letters available for mutation. This means the totality of mutations are likely to be unique for each individual and/or for each genetic line.

This means that each individual carries a unique set of mutations in their Y chromosome and mtDNA that can be related to specific ancestral lines that represent ancestors in the recent and distant past.

The numbers of mutations are predicable in large part per generation and by sophisticated data analysis can be tracked back in time by using an average number of years per generation and cross referencing individuals that have in common some portion of mutations allowing genetic lines to be discerned. This analysis (of Y chromosome and mtDNA) has produced astounding results.

The echo of historical events including wars, dispersions, migrations and population collapses can be tracked when a 6,000 year time frame is assumed instead of the 200,000 or so year time frame used by evolutionists.

The echo of the effects of the global Genesis flood die off and the dispersal from the Tower of Babel are clear in the genetic record along with many historical facts recorded; also in other documents.

Of course, by now it should be clear that the millions of years needed by evolution is problematical given the more deleterious effects of accumulated random mutations leading to the demise of more and more critters. This is compounded by the much higher mutation rate than previously believed due to rates as determined by contemporary populations and cleaner, more accurate DNA analysis.

Ironically, given what we know, the 'survival of the fittest' will be those individuals with fewer mutations, generally speaking, helping to attenuate the devolution process.

By appropriate shuffling of autosomal DNA (DNA contributed by both parents), Adam and Eve had all the information needed to create every unique human being in existence. The fall complicated things a bit with random mutations and other genomic issues we may not yet know about, but I suspect the DNA of our resurrection bodies will be in a pre-fall state.

Note: mutations can also (and probably often do) occur with each new cell division during normal metabolism as cells age, occurring millions of times each day. These copying errors could explain many symptoms of aging as they accumulated in each cell line of the tens of trillions of cells in each adult human. This would limit the effectiveness of anti-aging strategies (in my opinion). (Perhaps telomeres are not the age limiting factor once believed.)

Chapter 6 The First Covenant

And let them have <u>dominion</u> over the fish of the sea, and over the fowl of the air, and over the cattle, and over all the earth, and over every creeping thing that creepeth upon the earth. Genesis 1:26b- (KJV, emphasis mine)

And God blessed them, and God said unto them, Be fruitful and multiply, and fill the earth, and subdue it: and have <u>dominion</u> over the fish of the sea and over the fowl of the air, and over every living thing that moveth upon the earth. Genesis 1:28 (mine, emphasis mine)

Prior to this point God assumed all authority over His creation and could legally (justly) exercise His sovereignty in any matter without conflict. However, morality aside, at this point He gave dominion over all the earth to humanity; thus leaving discretion to humanity over decisions related to the governing, control and actions affecting the earth.

And to every beast of the earth, and to every fowl of the air, and to every thing that creepeth upon the earth, wherein there is life, I have given every green herb for meat: and it was so. And God saw every thing that He had made, and, behold, it was very good. And the evening and the morning were the sixth day.

Thus the heavens and the earth were finished, and all the host of them. Genesis 1:30,31;2:1 (KJV)

At this point God's creation was perfect (very good), a living paradise, complete with the means (provision) to continue into perpetuity, without strife or pleading or any kind of lack or suffering and humanity was given complete dominion over all the earth. Death and predation did not exist in this original perfect creation of God's plan.

And the Lord God commanded the man, saying, Of every tree of the garden thou mayest freely eat:

But of the tree of the of the knowledge of good and evil, thou shalt not eat of it: for in the day that thou

eatest thereof thou shalt surely die. Genesis 2:16-17 (KJV)

This was the first covenant between God and Man. A covenant, Biblically speaking, is a binding agreement where a violation of such must result in death of the violating party. The interesting thing to note about this covenant is that the violation by disobedience would result in death whether or not the covenant was in effect since death is actually separation (and not non-existence) from God.

There was only one restriction placed upon Adam and Eve; that they would not eat of the tree of the knowledge of good and evil.

It seems the only things they would lack would be fear, anxiety and conflict. Their destiny would be peaceful existence, joy, happiness, expansion and prosperity under the loving gaze of their Creator.

And Adam said, This is now bone of my bone and flesh of my flesh: she shall be called Woman, because she was taken out of Man.

Therefore shall a man leave his father and his mother, and shall cleave unto his wife: and they shall be one flesh.

And they were both naked, the man and his wife, and they were not ashamed. Genesis 2:23-25 (KJV)

Somehow Adam and Eve were ONE in the beginning; and God separated them for the purpose of companionship and pro creation and divided them such that they complimented each other and were irresistibly attracted to each other; to become one flesh again and to learn what it was to fall in love and share life together as one; to have children that would have the experience of love like their own in their own future.

Thus God, from the very beginning, established Marriage as between a man and a woman and to be the source of future generations in the form of children. This so called nuclear family is the very foundation of human existence, providing stability, continuity, and identity to individuals and society as a whole; from the very beginning of humanity and time itself. Selah.

Perhaps there is another thing they would lack and that is appreciation of their complementarity, destiny and how good they had it and the Love and Goodness of their Holy God.

God gave them free will so that they could worship and love Him of their own free will. Free will implies choice. They would have the opportunity to exercise their option if given a choice, otherwise they could only be robots, even having self awareness.

Free will is a secret ingredient to give meaning to life and the infinity of God is shown in His ability to give meaning to life eternally, without end.

And the four beasts had each of them six wings about him; and they were full of eyes within: and they rest not day and night, saying, Holy, holy, holy, Lord God Almighty, which was, and is, and is to come. Revelation 4:8 (KJV)

At each iteration the four beasts would perceive a new aspect of the nature of God never before seen, causing them to repeat their prayer of praise. Heaven will never be boring.

Chapter 7 Their Human Descendants

Both creationists and secularists agree that there was a genetic Adam and a genetic Eve.

As of this writing secularists assert that Adam never knew Eve and all other genetic lines died off over a 200,000 year (or so) period of time. (It is my understanding that some secularists have given up on the 200,000 year timeline given the coherence afforded by the 6,000 year timeline.)

The Bible clearly stats that Adam and Eve knew each other and were the sole source of the human family tree and lived about 6,000 years ago.

Adam and Eve were our first and most ancient ancestors.

Be fruitful, and multiply, and fill the earth, Genesis 1:28b (mine)

And from Adam came Seth (paternal line)
and from Seth came Enos
and from Enos came Cainan
and from Cainan came Mahalaleal
and from Mahalaleal came Jared
and from Jared came Enoch
and from Enoch came Methuselah
and from Methuselah came Lamech
and from Lamech came Noah

This genealogy is detailed in Genesis 5:3-29. All of the above are our ancestors in the paternal line from Adam to Noah since the Genesis flood obliterated all other paternal genetic lines up to that point. This is astounding. We can all trace our family tree for the first ten generations along our paternal line from Adam to Noah.

The Genesis Flood was a global flood and caused a major collapse of the human population. This is detectable in both the paternal and maternal lines by virtue of the latest genetic research made possible by the presence of mutations in the DNA code that are in totality unique in each individual, propagated and accumulated in each succeeding generation's germ line unto the present.

And the Lord said, I will destroy man whom I have created from the face of the earth; both man, and beast, and the creeping thing, and the fowls of the air; for it repenteth me that I have made them.
But Noah found grace in the eyes of the Lord. Genesis 6:7-8 (KJV)

Indeed, the geological record, when analyzed from a Biblical World View, gives powerful evidence of a catastrophe beyond human imagination.

For example: (3) Near the end of the Genesis flood, after new mountain ranges formed, when things were starting to calm down there was an earth quake so powerful that a mountain range in Southern California that was 12 miles by 12 miles, the Kingston Range, was ripped from its foundation and bounced along for 60 miles, where geologists found it at its final resting place.

The 12 x 12 mile range was still above the floor of the plain at its final resting place, attesting to its recent arrival; otherwise over millions of years its weight would have sunk it into the surrounding plain; never to be seen again.

They were able to trace it back to where it came from, 60 miles eastwards. The origin of the 12 x 12 range was identified by the foundation below the surface of the surrounding plain left behind when the above ground portion was ripped from its foundation…

Catalina Island is believed to have a similar history, originating on land and ending up in the ocean.

But also if ye shall say unto this mountain, Be thou removed, and be thou cast into the sea; it shall be done. Matthew 21:21d (KJV)

This is not to say that Matthew 21:21 refers to the Genesis flood but to say that from God's point of view this is not hyperbole. We don't have to downgrade what the Bible says to a humanist perspective. **In fact that kind of thinking can lead to a non-Biblical world view.**

Many people are interested in tracing their genealogy through submitting their DNA samples to companies that perform various analysis of their gnome to provide this data, but not all analyze the mtDNA and Y chromosomes.

The most recent mtDNA and Y chromosome research actually allows (in many cases) tracing all the way back to Noah, Noah's sons and three daughter in-laws given the proper focus of analysis performed by the company providing the analysis. By virtue of the Biblical genealogies and maternal and paternal DNA information (available in every cell of each individual) every individual could trace all the way back to Adam and Eve.

This analysis is likely to improve over time assuming that additional DNA samples become available to trace some of the more obscure genetic lines from the present backwards to common ancestors in the recent and remote past.

These genetic lines tracing back from the present, from theoretically every individual person on the planet gives strong evidence of population dynamics, of mass migrations and dispersals like Babel, mass dies offs like the Genesis flood, wars and famines in the echoes of the DNA evidence in paternal and maternal lines revealing the historicity of the Bible in unprecedented manner.

(Note: by submitting samples related to DNA analysis to various companies you may be giving up important rights to your own DNA molecule; your DNA code may be sold to other entities or governments to do with what they will. Perhaps there are ethical services available or one will rise up to fill the need. Check the terms and conditions if you like. Be discrete in your inquiries since there are those who would restrict such knowledge given how it would be used).

The best information for genetic testing can be found in Appendix C of Dr. Jeanson's book 'Traced'.

Chapter 8 Fall and Redemption

And the LORD God commanded the man, saying, Of every tree of the garden thou mayest freely eat: But of the tree of the knowledge of good and evil, thou shalt not eat of it: for in the day that thou eatest thereof thou shalt surely die. Genesis 2:16-17 (KJV)

Now the serpent was more subtle than any beast of the field which the Lord God had made. And he said unto the woman, Yea, hath God said, Ye shall not eat of every tree of the garden? Genesis 3:1 (KJV)

The serpent by what he said "Yea, hath God said, Ye shall not eat of every tree of the garden?" gave a negative spin to what God originally said by leaving out the positive aspect "Of every tree of the garden thou mayest freely eat" and the most negative aspect of what God said "thou shalt surely die". The serpent was being deceptive from the get go.

But I fear, lest by any means, as the serpent beguiled Eve through his subtlety, so your minds should be corrupted from the simplicity that is in Christ. 2 Corinthians 11:3 (KJV)

The word simplicity above refers to the plain reading of scripture, which is what the satan wants to obscure. This tactic is so common that it has been given the nickname of 'Genesis 3 attack' by some. Simply stated the tactic is one where doubt is cast upon the word of God by subtle or not so subtle paraphrasing, deletions or outright corruption of what is said in the word of God by reinterpretation using imaginary contextual synthesis in order to say something that is not even implied in scripture…

One example of this is the so called 'gap theory' which was proposed to insert billions of years into the Biblical narrative to satisfy theoretical needs of the now obsolete theory of biological macro evolution among others. Repent.

Another example is in Matthew 4:6 where the satan omits "to keep thee in all thy ways" from Psalm 91:11 (KJV).)

Eventually, in the Genesis narrative, Eve capitulates to the solicitation of the devil and eats of the fruit of the tree of the knowledge of good and evil; and Adam follows suit.

And when the woman saw that the tree was good for food, and that it was pleasant to the eyes, and a tree to be desired to make one wise, she took of the fruit thereof, and did eat, and gave also unto her husband <u>with her</u>; and he did eat. Genesis 3:6 (emphasis mine, KJV)

She succumbed to the three classes of temptations:
    'lust of the flesh',
    'lust of the eyes' and
    'the pride of life'.

And we do not need to glorify Adam's response; though he was there with her, he raised no objection. Thus the fall was total and its fact legally indisputable, giving the satan authority over the earth and humanity ***because they obeyed the satan and disobeyed God.***

And the eyes of them both were opened, and they knew they were naked; and they sewed fig leaves together, and made themselves aprons. Genesis 3:7 (KJV)

Immediately, the death predicted by God comes to pass. That is spiritual death of both Adam and Eve. They were disconnected from the Spirit of God, which they had shared with God prior to the fall.

Eve was deceived while Adam knew what he was doing. Perhaps he loved Eve so much he was willing to make such a sacrifice to be with her or it was peer pressure. Regardless, had it not been so there would have been no offspring, no human race and none of us. Perhaps.

The intimate connection of God's Spirit with all of creation would have to suffer as it would make no sense to maintain a perfect paradise of a cosmos in light of the fall of the pinnacle of God's creation: humanity. This is implied by the Genesis narrative regarding God's curse following the fall.

Cursed is the ground for thy sake; Genesis 3:17c (KJV)

For we know that the whole creation groaneth and travaileth in pain together until now. Romans 8:22 (KJV)

Importantly, the action of Adam and Eve, by their betrayal of God, gave dominion over the earth to the satan and by the fact of God's unconditional delegation of authority over the earth to Adam and Eve (and humanity by inheritance) God could not legally directly interfere with their decision from God's authority by His spoken word. He could not speak Jesus into existence like He did Adam. This would have violated that first covenant.

Instead, God would have to use humans to speak His words to effect a Savior into existence to wrest the authority given to the satan back to humanity. As we now know this would take some time and involve many imperfect prophets. Eventually Jesus would be manifest in the flesh:

The LORD thy God will raise up a Prophet from the midst of thee, of thy brethren, like unto me; unto Him ye shall hearken;

I will raise them up a Prophet from among their brethren , like unto thee, and will put my words in His mouth; and He shall speak unto them all that I shall command him. Deuteronomy 18:15,18(KJV)

Therefore the Lord Himself shall give you a sign; Behold, a virgin shall conceive, and bear a son, and shall call his name Immanuel. Isaiah 7:14 (KJV)

Humanity was now fallen and each individual born of the flesh would be born spiritually dead, in that their spirit would not be 'connected' to God (except for Jesus).

One could say that Adam and Eve were given a choice to deny God (from their connected state) and their children are given a choice to accept God's salvation (from their disconnected state).

And I will put enmity between thee and the woman, and between thy seed and her seed; it shall bruise thy head, and thou shalt bruise His heal. Genesis 3:15 (KJV)

An incredibly terse verse, Genesis 3:15 sets the stage for the salvation of humanity and reveals important details that become obvious in scripture:

1) Lucifer and Eve would be enemies;

2) and so would sons of Lucifer and her descendent, Jesus;

But now ye seek to kill me,

And Jesus said unto them, If God were your Father, ye would love me: for I proceeded forth and come from God; neither came I of myself, but he sent me.

Ye are of your father the the devil, and the lusts of your father ye will do. John 8:40a,42,44a (KJV)

3) Lucifer would suffer a fatal blow to the head in that he would loose his authority over humanity, the earth and

death, experience complete defeat because of what Jesus did on the cross;

After this, Jesus knowing that all things were now accomplished, that the scripture might be fulfilled, saith I thirst.

When Jesus therefore had received the vinegar, he said, It is finished: and he bowed His head, and gave up the ghost. John 19:28,30 (KJV)

4) and Jesus being both man and God and sinless, would suffer injustice, physical torture, physical death and spiritual agony and by Lucifer's loss of authority (by virtue of Jesus' sinlessness) and the bodily resurrection of Jesus would Jesus ultimately have victory by restoring authority to humanity and by virtue of Jesus' humanity share the authority over the earth with those who are born of the Spirit and submitted to His will.

5) Thus salvation would be realized; salvation being the work of God; (by grace; an unearned gift from Jesus) through faith.

For all have sinned, and come short of the glory of God;

Being justified freely by His grace through the redemption that is in Christ Jesus;

For the wages of sin is death; but the gift of God is eternal life through Jesus Christ our Lord.

That if thou shalt confess with thy mouth the Lord Jesus, and shalt believe in thine heart that God hath raised him from the dead, thou shalt be saved. Romans 3:23,24;6:23;10:9(KJV)

Wherefore, as by one man sin entered into the world, and death by sin; and so death passed upon all men, for that all have sinned: Romans 5:12 (KJV)

Therefore as the offense of one unto all men to condemnation; even so by the righteousness of one the free gift came   upon all men unto justification of life. Romans 5:17 (KJV)

For since by man came death, by man came also the resurrection of the dead.

For as in Adam all die, even so in Christ shall all be made alive.

And so it is written, The first man Adam was made a living soul; the last Adam was made a quickening spirit.1 Corinthians 15:21-22, 45 (KJV)

Thus the first Adam sinned and affected all with death and the last Adam, Jesus, provided for salvation of all with His one sacrifice to those who accept His gift.

(The fallen must accept His gift in order to receive it otherwise they would have been saved without a choice. They would still have to choose continued salvation or choose spiritual death as Adam and Eve chose. This would be an interminable situation like Adam and Eve had to face in order to allow the rest of us choose life one time for all eternity rather than having to continue without choice until one chose to choose death. While this remains a mystery this is why things unfolded the way they did in my opinion.)

Starting with Genesis 4 and all the way to Revelation 22, the will of God being played out would be revealed in the historical narrative, giving account in an unprecedented manner to include future events along with past and present with uncanny accuracy that only the God we know is capable of: an accurate historical narrative of the future before it happens.

The gift to believers of the word of God in the form of the Bible is the gift of truth, past, present and to come, seems unavailable to unbelievers by virtue of their unbelief, a sad thing indeed.

The book of Isaiah, penned long before the crucifixion, with an almost 100% intact copy (and accurate to the 1000AD version) found with the dead sea scrolls dated to about 200BC give many prophetic accounts, so much so that secular scholars reject its account because they believe it to be impossibly accurate. The prophecies include an account of the crucifixion here in part:

He is despised and rejected of men; a man of sorrows, and acquainted with grief, and we hid as it were our faces from Him; He was despised, and we esteemed Him not.

Surely He hath borne our griefs, and carried our sorrows: yet we did esteem Him stricken, smitten of God, and afflicted.

But He was wounded for our transgressions, He was bruised for our iniquities: the chastisement of our peace was upon Him; and with His stripes we are healed. Isaiah 53:3-5 (KJV)

Finally, having reestablished internal connection with the Father, Son and Holy Ghost, the believer has within, God in the person of the Holy Spirit who comforts and guides the believer through the impossible challenges facing Christians wanting to live a sanctified life through Christ in this fallen world. Note: following being born again, the believer should petition for the baptism of the Holy Spirit to obtain access to Pentecostal benefits. Note: the believer should also seek water baptism to declare ones commitment to the Lordship of Jesus and rinsing away the 'old man' residue. Then the believer should pursue discipleship in order to reach maturity in Christ to be able to guide and counsel baby Christians thru to maturity in Christ.

According as His divine power hath given unto us all things that pertain unto life and godliness, through the knowledge of Him that hath called us to glory and virtue:

Whereby are given unto us exceeding great and precious promises: that by these ye might be partakers of the divine nature, having escaped the corruption that is in the world through lust. 2 Peter 1:3-4 (KJV)

Amen and amen.

Chapter 9 Evil Overwhelms

From the time of Adam who lived 930 years until Noah, society became preoccupied with evil until God's plan for salvation was threatened in that if things continued in the current trend there would be no virgins for Jesus to be born of.

It is obvious that God was not micromanaging affairs on the earth, though immorality was still Gods issue to deal with fall or no fall. Cain was cursed but also protected. Man eventually took this to mean sin was ok.

This was not the only problem. There were fallen angels and giants upon the earth. Hybrids were in existence. Part human part angel. This is my opinion. Others have different interpretations of scripture in this regard. I am not interested in defending my opinion. I hold it because of scripture combined with the understanding of the total catastrophe of the Genesis flood that I believe God was dealing with more than human sin. I believe the gene pool was corrupted intentionally in defiance of Divine Law (and there was perhaps DNA technology beyond what we have today). Can one think of a greater crime against God?

During the flood the earth was nearly cracked in two and (3) completely resurfaced and the continents galloped to their current positions upon the breaking of the earth's crust, resulting in tsunamis every hour or so that covered the land masses, depositing miles deep sediments rapidly covering millions upon millions of living creatures including dinosaurs that were rapidly fossilized due to being covered by sediment before they could decay or be eaten.

Fossils are normally a rarity because dead animals are eaten and remains decay before they can be buried by natural processes. The fossils that are found world wide were buried around 4,500 years ago, rather than the 65 million years as proposed by secular geologists. Evidence for this is found in recent finds by secular geologists that many or most dinosaur fossils still contain biological tissues that show that the fossils are of recent origin. This includes cartilage, blood vessels and red blood cells that can easily be seen in a microscope. Carbon 14 testing also attests to the youthfulness of fossils and everything else from diamonds to petroleum.

Note that the age of the earth as being millions and billions of years old was proposed.in order to try to establish an earth old enough to provide enough time for macro evolution, where one kind of animal morphs into another, like dinosaurs evolving into birds. We now know enough about genetics that this proposal is ridiculous.

There are many so called scientific theories that have been falsified in fact, but still clung to for various reasons. The lesson here should be obvious in that the Bible is the superior source of information and should not be subjugated to current scientific fads.

There were giants in the earth in those days; and also after that, when the sons of God came in unto the daughters of men, and they bare children to them, the same became mighty men which were of old, men of renown.

And God saw that the wickedness of man was great in the earth, and that every imagination of the thoughts of his heart was only evil continually.

But Noah found grace in the eyes of the LORD. Genesis 6:4-5,8 (KJV)

I will not repeat the story of Noah's ark, but I believe evidence suggests it is absolutely true as told in the Genesis account. The ark is the first historical Biblical artifact discovered as I understand it. (4) The remains are located in the Mountains of Ararat in Turkey as stated in the Bible:

And the ark rested in the seventh month, on the seventeenth day of the month, upon the mountains of Ararat. Genesis 8:4 (KJV)

But not on Mount Ararat as others state. (Mountains of Ararat is not the same as Mount Ararat).

After the flood the human gene pool was reduced to one male (Noah) and three females (wives of the son's of Noah).

The analysis of DNA mutations agree with these facts. The mtDNA shows a collapse to three maternal genetic lines at 4500 years, the time of the Genesis flood, and a single source at 6000 years (Eve to be specific).

The analysis of the Y chromosome shows a collapse to one genetic line at 4500 years, (Noah to be specific).

These timelines do NOT contradict the most recent secular findings to date.

Chapter 10 Noah and Beyond

This is a book about Adam and Eve and their descendants. Their descendants span the whole of existence of the human race up to the present. Therefore there is more to explore of the intersection of Biblical historical accounts with current DNA research and relevant extra-Biblical historical documents.

It should be understood that the DNA research of Dr. Jeanson reveals many details of human history that is corroborated with Biblical and non-Biblical historical documents. This clarifies historical events by adding indispensable details of genetic lines of descent impacted by various population changes and movements of specific people groups over time.

Dr. Jeanson has shown that the Y chromosome mutation accumulation (of 3 mutations per generation and a 25 year generational average and a 4500 year time span) within the human genome of living persons correlate with documented population statistics on both a global and regional basis.

Using a benchmark of externally determined population counts provides the framework for a means to test model hypothesis against an UNBIASED dataset.

The significance of this research cannot be exaggerated. It will likely spawn a whole new interest around genetic testing at least for believers, Jews and Mormons.

Establishing relative linages is one thing, it is another thing all together to be able to relate those linages to the Biblical account of historical events. Since the Bible's relevance is denied by secularists (in large part) they do not appreciate what we have.

This research will likely continue into perpetuity to flesh out more details not otherwise assessable by any other means.

While the technical details are a real deep dive into PHD land, with what we already know we should be able to trace individuals from the present through the sons of Jacob (Israel) (or other parallel genetic lines) through the sons of Noah to Noah (which implies Adam).

An individual's (his or hers) most recent paternal Y chromosome's mutations can reveal the exact genetic linage for that individual with amazing detail going from the present to the past once the 'past' is appropriately ascertained and linages firmly established. This discernment process is already underway.

We should be able to add to our knowledge of Biblical events and our understanding of the impact of those events on observed phenomena we see today.

When certain events occurred helps to confirm the accuracy of the Biblical account. (Such as the famine in Egypt and the migration of Jacob's family to Egypt, the Exodus, the entry of the Israelites into the promised land, the Tower of Babel dispersal.)

Furthermore, the impact of certain events upon populations and their genetic makeup will help to explain how and why the human race is the way it is as we know it today.

It is perhaps ironic that these copying errors (DNA mutations), a symptom of the fall, gives us such powerful tools to supplement our understanding of the Biblical account of our ancestry.

Chapter 11 Population Collapse

The Biblical account in Genesis 10 reveals a major population collapse of all land creatures at about 4500 years ago. It is from this point that genetic diversity observed today must be explained. This includes animals and humans.

It is my contention that this diversity arose in a mere 4500 years and did NOT arise from macro evolution due to mutations and natural selection over millions of years. Because of the claims made by evolutionists over the last hundred years or so, most people would disagree with this statement.

But note: in chapter 6 it was established that, due to the overwhelming statistical likelihood of deleterious mutations above beneficial mutations, mutations would result in devolution and eventual extinction of all critters given enough time. There would be more mutations than a species could tolerate.

Secularists recognize that such a limit exists but account for a much slower mutation rate, which is completely unsupported by high quality DNA analysis of living subjects. Their theoretical foundation rely on ancient DNA (subject to decay) and cherry picking of contemporary samples to fit their expectations.

DNA research supports a 4500 year time frame. The details of how diversity arose in such a short time is beyond this scope, but a 30,000 foot view suggests that genomic design in general (both human and animal) is such that genetic possibilities exist within DNA that are not necessarily expressed in a given individual but are passed on to offspring for later consideration. Within any mating pair there exist billions or more viable genetic combinations preprogrammed within the germ cells that combine at the moment of conception.

While population collapse itself does not result in diversification but rather limits diversification due to the loss of specific genetic lines by the collapse, it is population isolation that leads to visible ethnic like characteristics taking root in a population by, paradoxically, reduction of genetic possibilities due to isolation. This is why we don't all look like Adam and Eve and Chihuahuas don't give birth to Doberman Pinschers.

Mutations do have some impact as it has been pointed out that some of the diversity in dogs is the result of damaged genes resulting from semi-random mutations (recent finding indicate some parts of a genome are more or less susceptible to mutations so it is not purely random).

So, the Genesis flood sets the stage for the onset of diversification that we see today but not the actual diversification. That occurs a little later, for Humanity, at the time of the Tower of Babel dispersal as documented in Genesis 11.

Chapter 12 One Language

And the whole earth was of one language, and of one speech. Genesis 11:1 (KJV)

Regardless of the situation regarding language before the Genesis flood it is obvious that there would be one language in use after the flood due to only one human family surviving the flood, consisting of Noah, his wife and Noah's three sons and their wives, eight individuals.

The obvious question therefore is threefold, given one extended family only 4500 years ago with one language:

1. Where did all of the languages we see today come from?

Go to, let us go down, and there confound their language, that they may not understand one another's speech. Genesis 11:7 (KJV)

It is safe to assume that within family groups speech would still be understandable, but by this time there would be enough people (family) groups, resulting in a significant number of separate languages as we perceive today.

While there are thousands of dialects today, there are approximate 70 language types matching the approximate 70 families at the time of the dispersion.

2. Where did all of the human diversity seen today come from?

And from thence did the LORD scatter them abroad upon the face of all the earth. Genesis 11:9b (KJV)

The scattering of the people groups led to the diversification of the human species.

By this time (since the Genesis flood) there were several generations since Noah, as is documented in Genesis 11:10-19, from Shem to Peleg. The implication is there would be small groups of people (extended families) scattered, an ideal situation genetically speaking to result in unique genetic characteristics specific to each small isolated group.

Thus diversity would literally appear in the physical characteristics of the individuals of each isolated group as we see them today.

3. Where did the eight billion people on the earth today come from?

According to the genealogy accounts in Genesis 10 and the first part of Genesis 11 (prior to Peleg) the population was expanding rapidly each generation. Each husband and wife were having many children.

After the Tower of Babel dispersal the population grew very slowly for about 4,000 years as can be seen in the population curves derived from historical documents (see Color Plate 230 in the book "Traced" by (Dr.) Nathaniel T. Jeanson).

Suddenly, around 1700 AD the population grew at a fantastic rate, growing from less than a billion people before 1700 AD to the eight billion people in less than 400 years.

So it seems it took about 4,000 years for the human species to recover from the effects of the scattering and isolation caused by the Tower of Babel dispersal.

Chapter 13 One Breeding Pair

Given that Noah's ark held only one pair of non-domestic stock of each given kind of animal, where did all of the species of each kind arise from (in such a short time span)?

It seems plausible that after disembarking from Noah's ark following the flood, the non-domestic animals would have migrated from the resting place of the ark, breeding along the way.

They would have scattered as per God's command over time. Small groups or herds would become stationary according to the accommodations provided by the environments they found themselves in.

Available food and nesting sites would have limited their population in a given area and the excess critters would have continued expanding outward seeking accommodations according to their needs.

The result would have been small populations of isolated animal groups of a given kind; and due to Genetic specialization from isolation of available genetic traits in a population (known as genetic drift) and natural selection; leading to speciation. Note this process is not macro evolution. You would never see a dog producing a litter containing cats. They would still all be dogs no matter how different they may appear. Wings or feathers would not suddenly appear, neither would fins as these changes would require the coordinated manifestation of many new genetic functions that are impossible to attain given the random incidents of germ cell mutations over extreme periods of time.

Another factor impacting the mix of breeds and their final locations would have been the settling out of the landscape and climate following the devastation of the Genesis flood (a global flood).   Sea level changes would open and close migration paths as sea levels changed caused by the ice age that occurred after the flood.

It is my understanding that there has been only one time in earth's history where the climate changed drastically enough to cause an ice age. That would be the Genesis flood, due to volcanoes of unprecedented quantity and geysers spewing hot sea water from the mantle 60 miles high from a ring of broken crust 50,000 miles long, "the ring of fire" as is referred to today.

Though mutations might have an impact on speciation, in general speciation results from genetic isolation (as is understood by dog breeders for instance) and natural selection. Mutations would still lean strongly to the deleterious side of the equation and never result in new viable genetic functions or new animal kinds.

The most recent DNA research reveals that most if not all of the human genome is functional. There appears to be no 'junk' DNA in the genome. The viral like structures (so-called endogenous retroviruses) discovered in the genome appear to be functional and necessary components to make life possible therefore they are not evolutionary ancestral artifacts regardless of how similar they may be to such.

These structures in actuality provide immunity from many harmful external viruses. That endogenous retrovirus appear in multiple species is purely functional and the source is not inheritance from evolutionary processes.(Though it is known that genetic material does at times migrate horizontally across different micro organisms. I am not aware of this phenomenon happening with multicellular organisms, but it can't be ruled out.)

It should be noted that these endogenous DNA fragments in many cases are not really identical in structure to retroviruses and are found to be functional and therefore have been mischaracterized by evolutionary biologists as has much of the extant DNA from the early days of 'junk' DNA.

Furthermore, the human genome, even where similar to other species, has been found to function differently and at a higher level than is found in those other species.

Chapter 14 The Rest of the Story

DNA is part of a language system used to implement living organisms. This language system has a lot in common with computer language systems used to implement computer processes in use today.

As a software developer of over 35 years I see behind the scenes of DNA as it appears in living systems. In computer language systems there are several components necessary to make a computer language effective and useful.

There is the actual computer code used directly by the computer to perform some process. In living systems there is DNA found in the cell that codes for some process needed by the living cell to maintain life.

These processes may code for specific proteins or may code for a variety of regulatory functions, directing the development or maintenance of the cells and organism in general. This stuff is very very complicated and not well understood. (It makes one pause and consider what these mRNA vaccines are really doing inside the body. And yet there is almost no testing done before they are mandated. Yikes!)

As a programmer, if I want to come up with a new computer process (app), I would retrieve from a library of program modules and arrange them according to the need and code a bit more logic to specialize the resultant program to perform as needed by the specification provided.

DNA is no different. We might not have visibility of the actual library of preprogrammed models for common use, but we could see those modules in different apps or DNA in different organisms as they had common functions to perform.

As a programmer, I would never create a new program from scratch once I had a library of useful modules to choose from as the modules would have been tested and working, saving me a lot of time and effort, resulting in a much more reliable process whether it be an app or a living creature.

For DNA, the library could exist in the mind of God. If you don't believe in God then life is impossible. Just ask any programmer wise enough to understand the problem. The same goes for synthetic organic chemists as life could not have arisen from pond scum because the purely chemistry part of the process would require many conflicting reactions to take place simultaneously within the space of the cell, leading to many chicken and egg type of problems.

It would seem that living organisms at any level could only come about fully functional and alive and complete in an instant. Not only is it necessary to construct the living organism in the proper way, it is also necessary establish the necessary state: a living being rather than an elegant corpse or a still birth. (For instance, when the egg and sperm unite to create a new living creature a mysterious flash of light is visible, marking the moment of time when a new living creature comes into existence, with its own unique DNA code.)

A computer gets its starting state established by a bootstrap routine. A living being gets its starting state by the breath of God.

Within a living cell it has been found that there are over 10 to the 78,000,000,000 ways to arrange the molecular bonds of various types in order to define the state of the cell and the cell is very particular about the way these bonds are arranged. It cannot be accidental and we, in our collective intelligence, cannot duplicate it. We do not even know where to start or what state is required.

Life has purpose and that purpose is for the greater bounds of the individual and community and not for the preservation of the genome as proposed in the "Selfish Gene" nor is the survival of the fittest the dictum upon which life is based. Our purpose is involved with our relationship with God, without Whom no real purpose is possible. We may have goals, dreams and aspirations but those are minor temporary waypoints and our ultimate destiny can only be achieved by actively seeking a real, personal, relationship with Jesus.

Epilogue

This work is the result of research begun in 2016 when the Holy Spirit told me to 'Prove the Bible'. Then I was told, while attending my first year of Bible College, in March of 2022, to write a book about Adam and Eve.

My journey to prove the Bible is an ongoing endeavor and will continue indefinitely into the future not because the Bible changes - it doesn't, but our knowledge in support of it does change, perhaps not as radically as science seems to change, but change it does.

In a way I have accomplished what I was directed to do in 2016. Initially, though I respected the Bible and had read it from back to front prior to 2016, I did not know how to take what I read. How much was reliable or intended to be historical fact or truly the word of God.

For me, I have firmly answered those questions. It is very very reliable, historically accurate and sacred; truly the word of God.

Much of what I found is beyond the scope of 'Adam and Eve'. So much has been discovered in recent times that I would be hard pressed to find any major Biblical account without substantial evidence in support of the Bible one way or the other.

References:

(1)Johns, W. H. (2016). Scriptural Geology, Then and Now. Answers Research Journal, 9, 317–337. https://answersresearchjournal.org/scriptural-geology-then-and-now/.

(2)Bergman, J. (2021). The History of Using Radiation to Speed Up Evolution. Answers Research Journal, 14, 61–66. https://answersresearchjournal.org/history-using-radiation-evolution/.

(3)Youtube"In-depth Explanation of What Caused Noah's Flood - Dr. Kurt Wise" from "In-Depth Creation Lectures (2017 IGH Conference)"

(4)Ron Wyatt, amateur archeologist, discoverer of many significant Biblical artifacts. Many believe what he reported and I am one, but since he was an amateur, professionals don't support his finds. Do your own research. It is fascinating. My opinion: he is the real deal.

(5)Nathaniel T. Jeanson (2021) Traced. (Human DNA's Big Surprise) ISBN 978-1-68344-291-2. This is a most significant work for the genetic basis for the historicity of Adam and Eve and by inference in support of the plain reading of Genesis 1 and 2.

(6)Nessy Carey, British Molecular Biologist, paraphrased from talk given at Royal Institute.

Notes

Notes